52 Weeks 52 Hikes
Journal:
Change Happens One Step At A Time

ISBN: 9781730745898

Welcome to the incredible community that has formed around 52 Weeks 52 Hikes.

You are about to embark on an incredible adventure of your very own making. Each 52 Week 52 Hike journey will be different. Hike your own hike.

Some people choose to do all of their hikes on one trail, some do all different trails. Some do one a week, some do multiple hikes in a week. Your journey, your rules.

Use the journal as you wish. Writing prompts are included, but feel free to ignore them. Blank space was included intentionally for the more artistic amongst us. Include a sketch or words. Or a sticker... that one was from my husband.

Turn the page, let's get started. Change happens one step at a time!

For more information visit us online at Tamis-Trippin.com

Follow 52 Weeks 52 Hikes on Facebook and Instagram and be sure and join our online community.

#52Weeks52Hikes

MY 52 WEEK 52 HIKE JOURNEY

On a whim, a friend and I decided to hike to Phantom Ranch in the Grand Canyon. Combined hiking experience between the two of us? Zero. Wine consumed between the two of us? More than zero.

The good news was that there was plenty of time to train. I signed up for a First Day Hike in North Alabama on January 1, 2016, which quickly morphed into what I began calling 52 Weeks 52 Hikes.

I finished my challenge on New Year's Eve 2016 at the Black Creek Trail in Gadsden, Alabama. Having logged many training miles on this system, I thought it was fitting for my 52nd hike.

In case you're wondering, I did make it to the Phantom Ranch, albeit solo, on December 2. More importantly, I made it back out.

It was tough. It was also incredible and life-changing. Looking up to the top of the canyon on the hike out had me wondering how I'd make it out of that big ditch, but then I'd look behind me and see how far I'd already come.

It's a lot like life, hiking, the only requirement is that you put one foot in front of the other over and over again. You've made the decision to begin, the hardest part is over.

I'm thrilled that you'll be joining the 52 Week 52 Hike community. I hope your path is filled with adventure.

See you on the trails!

Tami

Hike One
- Let's Go Outside!

Date _____ Trail _____

Length _____ Duration _____

How are you feeling? Excited? Nervous?

Goals for the day? Month? Year?

Hike Two
- Trust the magic of new
beginnings.

Date _____Trail_____

Length_____Duration_____

Highlights of the day:

Next time I will:

Hike Three
- You are an adventure story.

Date _____ Trail _____

Length _____ Duration _____

Today I experienced:

Challenges I faced:

Hike Four
- Out of all the paths you take, make sure some of them are dirt. - John Muir

Date _____Trail_____

Length_____Duration_____

Today I learned:

What fears do you have moving forward?

Hike Five
- It's okay to quit, just never on a bad day.

Date _____ Trail _____

Length _____ Duration _____

I feel like quitting when:

I keep going because:

Hike Six
- Chase your dreams.

Date _____Trail_____

Length_____Duration_____

My dream is:

I'll get there by:

Hike Seven
- One Step is Progress.

Date _____ Trail_____

Length_____ Duration_____

Progress I've made:

I would like to:

Hike Eight
- Hike Your Own Hike.

Date _____Trail_____

Length_____Duration_____

Challenges I face:

Spending time outdoors makes me feel:

Hike Nine
- Life is Better Outside.

Date _____ Trail _____

Length _____ Duration _____

Today I felt:

Tips or secrets for this trail:

Hike Ten
- Think less, live more.

Date _____Trail_____

Length_____Duration_____

I feel alive when:

Today my thoughts turned to:

Hike Eleven
- Congratulations! You've created a habit.

Date _____ Trail_____

Length_____ Duration_____

Compare this hike with Hike 1:

Have your goals changed or evolved?

Hike Twelve
- May your best miles be those covered on foot.

Date _____Trail_____

Length_____Duration_____

Benefits I've gain:

Advice I'd give to someone beginning:

Hike Thirteen
- May your search through nature lead you to yourself.

Date _____Trail_____

Length_____Duration_____

Today I heard:

This hike was:

Hike Fourteen
- Let your actions be louder than your words.

Date _____Trail_____

Length_____Duration_____

I want to:

To achieve that I will:

Hike Fifteen
- Let your dreams be bigger than your fears.

Date _____Trail_____

Length_____Duration_____

My fears are:

My dreams are:

Hike Sixteen
-The earth has it's music for those that will listen.

Date _____Trail_____

Length_____Duration_____

The hike was:

I heard:

Hike Seventeen
- Blessed are the curious for they shall have adventures.

Date _____Trail_____

Length_____Duration_____

My biggest adventure today was:

My biggest adventure so far:

Hike Eighteen
- Enjoy every moment.

Date _____ Trail _____

Length _____ Duration _____

Physically I felt:

Emotionally I felt:

Hike Nineteen
- Have stories to tell, not stuff to show.

Date _____Trail_____

Length_____Duration_____

Funniest thing that happened:

Biggest hiking fail so far:

Hike Twenty
- Almost halfway there!

Date _____ Trail _____

Length _____ Duration _____

Most beautiful thing I saw:

Today I feel:

Hike Twenty One
- Follow Your Heart.

Date _____Trail_____

Length_____Duration_____

At the halfway point I felt:

Strangest thing I saw:

Hike Twenty Two
- Ain't no stopping you now!

Date _____Trail_____

Length_____Duration_____

Trail description & conditions:

The hardest part was:

Hike Twenty Three
- Today is your greatest
adventure.

Date _____Trail_____

Length_____Duration_____

Today I learned:

I crushed it when:

Hike Twenty Four
- Mother Nature will lend you her power until you find your own.

Date _____Trail_____

Length_____Duration_____

I felt powerful when:

In nature I feel:

Hike Twenty Five
- Discomfort is the currency
used to achieve your goals.

Date _____Trail_____

Length_____Duration_____

I felt uncomfortable when:

I felt confident when:

Hike Twenty Six
- Halfway there, badass!

Date _____Trail_____

Length_____Duration_____

I have achieved:

I'd like to try:

Hike Twenty Seven
- Everything you want is on the other side of fear.

Date _____Trail_____

Length_____Duration_____

Fears I've overcome:

I'm still afraid of:

Hike Twenty Eight
- Comparison is the thief of
joy.

Date _____Trail_____

Length_____Duration_____

How I felt on my hike:

Trail description & weather conditions:

Hike Twenty Nine
- Keep Calm and Start Walking.

Date _____Trail_____

Length_____Duration_____

I felt calm when:

First thought when I arrived at my destination:

Hike Thirty
- Time you enjoy wasting is not wasted time.

Date _____ Trail_____

Length_____ Duration_____

I connected spiritually today by:

Nature has taught me:

Hike Thirty One
- Adopt the pace of nature,
her secret is patience.

Date _____Trail_____

Length_____Duration_____

I felt impatient when:

I felt happy when:

Hike Thirty Two
- Hiking - Best workout ever!

Date _____Trail_____

Length_____Duration_____

Physically I felt:

Fitness improvements I've seen:

Hike Thirty Three
- Just breathe.

Date _____ Trail_____

Length_____ Duration_____

The story of today was:

Next time I'll:

Hike Thirty Four
- The journey is the reward.

Date _____Trail_____

Length_____Duration_____

Looking back I:

Looking forward I:

Hike Thirty Five
- Be wild and free.

Date _____Trail_____

Length_____Duration_____

I felt free when:

I felt wild when:

Hike Thirty Six
- You are your only limit.

Date _____Trail_____

Length_____Duration_____

I feel limited when:

A challenge I overcame today:

Hike Thirty Seven
- Say yes to new adventures!

Date _____Trail_____

Length_____Duration_____

I felt great when:

When I finished I felt:

Hike Thirty Eight
- Believe you can and you're halfway there.

Date _____Trail_____

Length_____Duration_____

I felt confident when:

If I came back I would:

Hike Thirty Nine
- The best view comes after
the hardest climb.

Date _____Trail_____

Length_____Duration_____

How I felt physically:

How I felt emotionally:

Hike Forty
- Hello, adventure.

Date _____ Trail_____

Length_____ Duration_____

I wish I had:

I was surprised by:

Hike Forty One
- Dream. Believe. Do. Repeat.

Date _____Trail_____

Length_____Duration_____

I believe:

Describe the day:

Hike Forty Two
- Trust the journey.

Date _____Trail_____

Length_____Duration_____

I trust myself when:

I feet great when:

Hike Forty Three
- Every accomplishment begins with the decision to try.

Date _____Trail_____

Length_____Duration_____

I have accomplished:

I will try:

Hike Forty Four
- Almost there!

Date _____ Trail_____

Length_____ Duration_____

Compare today with Hike 1:

When I began today I felt:

Hike Forty Five
- You've got this.

Date _____Trail_____

Length_____Duration_____

This hike was incredible because:

Tell the story. Who you met, what
you experienced:

Hike Forty Six
- There are no straight lines in nature.

Date _____Trail_____

Length_____Duration_____

When I reached my destination I felt:

The most unexpected moment was:

Hike Forty Seven
- It always seems impossible until it's done - Nelson Mandela

Date _____Trail_____

Length_____Duration_____

When I begin this challenge I felt:

Today I felt:

Hike Forty Eight
- It doesn't matter how slowly you go, as long as you don't stop - Confucius

Date _____Trail_____

Length_____Duration_____

Did you ever feel like stopping?

I was happy to see:

Hike Forty Nine
- The best view comes after the hardest climb.

Date _____Trail_____

Length_____Duration_____

I was challenged today when:

My most challenging moment to date has been:

Hike Fifty
- There are no shortcuts to any place worth going -
Beverly Sills

Date _____Trail_____

Length_____Duration_____

How did this place make you feel?

It was worth it because:

Hike Fifty One
- Hiking and happiness go hand in hand or foot in boot
- Diane Spicer

Date _____Trail_____

Length_____Duration_____

I felt happy when:

To complete my goal I will:

Hike Fifty Two
- You did it!

Date _____Trail_____

Length_____Duration_____

Compare today with Hike 1:

What have you learned?

Did you achieve your goals? Did they
change?

What's next?

ABOUT THE AUTHOR

Tami Brooks completed her 52 Week 52 Hike journey in 2016 after deciding to hike to the Phantom Ranch in the Grand Canyon on a whim. She writes the blog Tami's Trippin' and is currently working on a book.

When she's not busy writing you can find her on the trail, in her kayak, or on the deck planning her next adventure.

Visit Tamis-Trippin.com to read more.

.

Made in the USA
Monee, IL
09 April 2022

94442244R00038